Copyright © 2018 by Ida Robinson

All rights reserved. This book or any portion thereof may not be reproduced or used in any manner whatsoever without the express written permission of the publisher except for the use of brief quotations in a book review or scholarly journal.

Inspiring Young Moms with a Vision
Nine Success Strategies for Young Moms with Big Dreams
Ida Robinson

© 2018 Ida Robinson
All Rights Reserved

Editing, Cover and Interior Design: SheEO Publishing Company
Illustration: Crystal Caraway, Fashionlistically Speaking
www.SheEOPublishing.com

First Printing 2018

ISBN #: 978-1-7335046-1-4

Disclaimer: The strategies provided in this book are personal growth recommendations and are not designed to substitute good judgment applicable to individual circumstances. The samples and examples are hypothetical and should not be taken as literal.

Published in the United States

INSPIRING YOUNG MOMS WITH A VISION

―――

Nine Success Strategies
for Young Moms with Big Dreams

Ida Robinson

To my father, Herbert M. Alston, continue to rest in paradise. My children Antonio, Charles, and Aniyah. My grandchildren Antonio and Charles, Jr. My one and only sister Eleathea "Leah" Robinson. My beautiful mother, Dorcas Robinson. My love Anthony Thomas. My nephews and a host of family and friends: I love you guys to the moon and back. You have supported me in more ways than one.

As parents, we're meant to help each other out and build each other up.
— Galit Breen, "Kindness Wins"

FOREWORD

By Ari Squires

Inspiring Young Moms with a Vision (IYMWV) is one of the most important books I've read this year. Ever mindful of the thriving world of literacy criticism, I recognize that this is a bold statement as IYMWV is Robinson's inaugural work. However, I make this proclamation with the same depth of conviction as my first reading of Vanzant's *Yesterday I Cried* and Nichol's *No Matter What!* undoubtedly recognizing authentic passion at first sight.

Reading the words found between these pages brought me a liberation that other works had not. So, despite Robinson's novice as a writer, or perhaps because of it, I consider her to be a breath of fresh air in the genre of self-help for millennial moms and IYMWV to be a powerful introduction to her flourishing career as a writer.

An empowerment coach and speaker by trade, Robinson shows us the importance of viewing life from a positive perspective. Using the style of the inspirational spectrum, she takes us on a journey through her personal story of troubling times of being a young mom and invites others in similar circumstances to examine the vision and possibility of their own lives.

As a scholar who is familiar with the works of Hemingway, Ellison and Nietzsche, I often encounter texts that make me consider who I *am* and the spaces I occupy in the world. Rarely, however do I come across a book that causes me to shift my inner awareness, forcing me to consider who I *was* and how phases of my being have guided me into spaces I now occupy. Inspiring Young Moms with a Vision did just that as it summoned self-examination and made me dig deeper into the aspects of my personal journey. Although I was not a young mom, I have had my fair share of feeling like the world is against me and trying times. So therefore the strategies in this book speak well to the woman who needs authentic guidance and support, which Robinson has so eloquently laid out for you.

Throughout this book, you will find, Robinson covers the gamut of the young mom's experience. She tackles self-love, low self-esteem, shifting your mindset and confronting all that comes with birthing new life. The weight of these topics has the innate ability to cast a shadow of darkness over an experiencer's life making it difficult to recognize their inherent light. But with Robinson's solutions, she lifts the weight which in turn, releases the potent negativity smothering a life by strengthening it with strong faith by providing strategies for developing a plan for success and living a life with purpose.

Inspiring Young Mom's with a Vision will transport you back to your reality and re-introduce you to the calling on your life both mentally and spiritually, on a different foot, with success tips to guide you. Further, I hope once you have read through its pages you will also declare it one of the most important books you've ever read and that all your *big* dreams come true.

Robinson says that you do not have to do life alone. And she has the tools to support you. Will you allow her to lead you? You're here right. I recommend you implement the nine steps to follow, so that you attract the abundance you envision and so rightfully deserve.

Ari Squires is the founder of Lend-a-Hand, Uplift-a-Child Foundation, and the author of *Release The Chains, All I See Is Possibility,* and *The Mindset of a SheEO.*

TABLE OF CONTENTS

FOREWORD vii

PREFACE xi

ACKNOWLEDGMENTS xiii

INTRODUCTION 1

SUCCESS STRATEGY #1
PARENTING WITH CONFIDENCE; SELF-VALUE/CORE PRINCIPLES 7
My Strategy #1 Notes 12

SUCCESS STRATEGY #2
ACKNOWLEDGING YOUR NEW REALITY;
MANAGING SUCCESS WHILE PARENTING 19
My Strategy #2 Notes 24

SUCCESS STRATEGY #3
WORK/LIFE BALANCE 31
My Strategy #3 Notes 36

SUCCESS STRATEGY #4
MANAGING YOUR MONEY; BUDGETING, SAVING, *NEED* VS. *WANT* 43
My Strategy #4 Notes 46

SUCCESS STRATEGY #5
SHIFTING FROM THE *I* MINDSET 53
My Strategy #5 Notes 60

SUCCESS STRATEGY #6
SELF-REFLECTION 67
My Strategy #6 Notes 69

SUCCESS STRATEGY #7
CREATING A DREAM BOARD 77
My Strategy #7 Notes 81

SUCCESS STRATEGY #8
CREATING YOUR ACTION PLAN FOR SUCCESS 89
My Strategy #8 Notes 94

SUCCESS STRATEGY #9
STEPS TO EXECUTING YOUR PLAN 101
My Strategy #9 Notes 105

ABOUT THE AUTHOR 113

PREFACE

I was inspired to write this book while expecting my second grandchild. The news also made me realize that this is a reality for many families: over 800,000 teens become pregnant each year in the United States alone. Supporting teen parents is the key to transforming our communities. If we shift our focus to creating successes rather than statistics out of young parents, we can not only help them succeed, but we can also contribute to reducing poverty in our society.

Success is not out of reach for teen parents. The options of owning a business, obtaining a degree, and achieving massive success are not out of reach. Continuing to dream big and live intentionally is important for teenaged parents. Setting goals and believing in their ability to accomplish them provides the inspiration to succeed beyond any circumstances.

Breaking the cycles of government dependency, school dropout, homelessness, and inadequate parenting skills will restore family unity and better the communities we serve as a whole.

While this book will be speaking to young moms from the heart of a former teen mom, the strategies covered serve as guidance for any mom and her supporters. I encourage any mom that is ready to break through mental blocks and successfully achieve her dreams to continue reading. You will be supplied with the tools you need to overcome and win.

ACKNOWLEDGMENTS

I would like to thank God: without you, nothing is possible.

I would like to acknowledge my big sister: you made sure your little sister was on point at all times, and I appreciate you.

I would like to acknowledge my aunts, Thomasine Alston and Latonya Robinson: you have both played a significant role in my life.

I would like to acknowledge Lynette Haywood and Linda Ingram: thank you so much; you guys played a major role in Charles's life, and I appreciate you.

I would like to acknowledge Anthony Thomas: you stepped in and played a significant role in my sons' lives in the absence of their dads (may they continue to rest in paradise).

I would also like to acknowledge my starting (5) for motivating me to be great.

INTRODUCTION

One of the most challenging obstacles many face in their lives is wanting to give up on themselves. Our burdens can become too unbearable. We grow weak mentally. We can become lost on our journey and feel there is no support for us. Even with all that I have lost and traumatic experiences I have been through, I cannot recall a moment where I wanted to give up on life, but there were many moments when I knew I wanted more. Before I get to how my life has changed by implementing a few strategies on my journey, I want to tell you about my life before I achieved success.

One critical moment was when I first found out that I was pregnant at sixteen. I was only in the tenth grade and was disappointed. I heard about girls my age either giving their babies up for adoption or aborting them. I knew in my heart that I did not want to do either of these things, but I still felt lost and confused.

Before becoming pregnant, I had planned to finish high school and go on to college. I grew up in the mean, cold streets of Washington, DC, and living in the projects for the rest of my life was not an option—at least not in my mind. When you grow up in an area surrounded by violence and poverty with drug-addicted parents, it's normal to seek a stable life. Being pregnant motivated me to want more for myself—and for my unborn child.

Life was not easy during my pregnancy, and certainly not any easier after I gave birth. Thankfully, my parents were supportive. However, there was one point in my life that was particularly hard on me. I remember it vividly. At the age of twenty—with two young kids—my father became ill. As his next of kin, because he and my mom were never married, I was the one who had to make the big decisions concerning his illness. At one point, he was hospitalized in a coma. Imagine that: a young mother of two facing all these life-and-death responsibilities and decisions. It was rough, but I'm here today mentoring hundreds of women and girls across the nation, so I guess I turned out alright. I'm here to share my story.

One night while my father was in the coma, I got a call from the hospital saying that they needed me to sign a few papers. I drove forty-five minutes to get there and was told that he needed a series of surgeries. The doctor pulled me into the hallway and told me that my father's organs were failing, and I should just pull the plug.

I stared at the doctor in horror. Here I was being told to let my father die. I knew I never could do that; this was the man who had supported me my entire life, and who I loved with all my heart. For the doctor to give up on him and ask me to do the same was despicable.

I stared directly into the doctor's eyes and asked him if my father's mind was still functioning properly. Looking reluctant to answer, he finally said that my father had all his mental faculties, but the machines were unable to make his other organs work. I nodded and declined to pull the plug on my father. A few weeks later, he woke up from his coma, and we were all happy for a while. My father passed away about nine months later when I was twenty-one, and three months after that, my mother suffered a stroke and was placed in a nursing home, where she remains to this day.

In less than a year, I lost both of my main supporters. I became the woman I am today because they taught me how to survive in spite of my circumstances. They taught me that family can persevere, no matter how hard the system tries to separate them.

I was a young mother taking care of two kids without my main support system. Once I came to grips with the fact that my dad was no longer there for me, and my mother was not physically able, I realized I had to put my big girl panties on and be the responsible parent and provider I needed to be. That was when I started digging deep within myself, wondering who I was and understanding what my values were, what was most important to me at that moment, and what decisions I had to make. I had to turn things around to ensure that my children and I could keep moving in the right direction, with or without my support system.

My decision-making went into overdrive. Not only did I have to be a supportive mom, I also had to be a supportive daughter. My mother had lost her best friend, and it took a toll on her health. She was residing in a nursing home, unable to do anything for herself.

While I was trying to maintain my sanity through all of this heartache and pain, I turned my grieving into beast mode as if I had no room to grieve properly. My entire life as I had known it had changed. My parents did not have any life savings, pension plans, or inheritance to pass down. I was now my biggest supporter and the sole provider for my family.

Some people can look at their parents and think: *Okay; I can fall and someone will be there to catch me.* Unfortunately, I no longer had that, so I had to search inside myself to understand where I was, the situation I was in, and what steps I needed to take to rise above a set of challenges that could stagnate me.

To free myself and my children, I reevaluated everything that was going on in my life and concluded that I had to move. I moved closer to my older sister so that my son could walk to school with my nephews while I was at work. We helped each other out a lot and became each other's support system.

It was around that time when I found out that my seven-year-old son had Attention Deficit Hyperactivity Disorder (ADHD). I would get a phone call from the school almost daily telling me what my son had done that day. I had to go to meeting after meeting, leaving work early. It got to a point where if I saw the school's number on the caller ID, I would cry, wondering what I was doing wrong. It was frustrating.

His teachers told me I needed to get him evaluated by a school psychologist. That was a really tough time in my life because I did not understand what he was going through and had no clue how to deal with it as a parent. I was still young and maturing, facing another tough decision. I eventually went to the school counselor, who recommended my son see a therapist.

I took him to three or four different doctors, who all told me that my son has ADHD. They all recommended I allow my son to take medication. That's when I realized I was my child's support system. I should have realized that when he was born, but I had allowed my parents to play such an important role in our lives that I was unaware of how much he needed me as his parent. I was so focused on pursuing the plans I had made prior to motherhood that I neglected being the attentive parent he needed. I found this out the hard way, once my parents were no longer there to help me.

When I had my strongest support system, I was able to think on and expand some of the things I wanted to do as a parent. I was able to work and go to school because I had my parents' support. I still had a plan to achieve my degree, but after losing my support system, I had to make some changes. This time it was bigger than my environment. It was time for a change in me. I needed to modify my strategy for success. I wasn't able to get my head straight until I moved near my sister and realized that I was my child's biggest cheerleader, and he needed me.

Because of those pivotal times, I'm living my life the way I want to now. I'm living in my purpose, and I'm able to help others. I'm working with my community to support young moms through personal and professional development, empowerment, and independence. I host leadership and social events for young girls, and I volunteer with organizations for many social issues affecting our community. I make a good income. I'm the business owner of Mom N' Powerment, which is an empowerment movement for moms.

Now, with the help of my family and from using a lot of the strategies I outline here, I have a good support system that allows me to have a great balance. I have two handsome sons and a beautiful daughter. I can work and live in my purpose. I've developed systems that help us to work together as a team. We respect each other and support each other in anything we want to do. A lot of these strategies have helped me achieve success in my life and have helped my relationship with my children. Their relationship to each other and our support system as a whole in the household works wonders for us. I've worked hard to get myself to this place in life, and my sole mission is to help others, including my own family.

My sister still helps us from time to time, and I help her whenever I can. My first son has come a long way from when he first was diagnosed with ADHD. I never once gave up, even when life was hitting me with all it had. I'm stronger for that, and I'm thankful every day that I can spend time with my kids and not have to worry about not having enough for them. I have a beautiful home that is filled with laughter and joy.

A lot of circumstances inspired me to write this book. One being that I was once where you are. I was that young mom trying to figure it all out, who did not have guidance from my parents to help me navigate through the rough patches of life, to know what exactly to do, and how to best position myself to succeed in life.

Now, I want to help you to succeed in life. By following these simple strategies, you, too, will be successful in life. You might feel like giving up, but don't. Life might throw some mighty heavy punches, but with perseverance and me as your support system, you can beat life at its own game.

These strategies are what helped me through the tough times, and I have never felt better for it. I will take you step-by-step through:

- parenting with confidence; establishing self-value/core principles;
- acknowledging your new reality of managing success while parenting;
- balancing work and family life;
- managing your money; budgeting, saving, needs vs. wants, and more;
- developing a new mindset; shifting from an I to a we success mindset;
- self-reflection;
- creating a dream board;
- creating your action plan for success;
- steps needed to execute your plan.

Follow these nine strategies, and you will succeed against the odds, but in your own way. Each of these strategies has a set of rules that must be followed for them to work to their full potential.

SUCCESS STRATEGY #1

PARENTING WITH CONFIDENCE; SELF-VALUE/CORE PRINCIPLES

Parenting is not as easy as it seems. You have more than just yourself to think about; you have someone else to look after as well, and in order to truly love another person, you must learn to love yourself.

I'm talking about self-love. Almost everything you do begins with how you see yourself and what you find valuable within yourself, including the decision to bring a child into the world. It all starts with you. You must have confidence in your ability to love yourself first before you can extend that love to someone else. That is one of the many reasons why I believe that practicing self-love is so important. No matter how you look at yourself and the values you have set out for yourself, if you don't have love for yourself, you sure can't deliver it to anyone else.

True, authentic success begins with self-love.

BELIEVING IN YOUR ABILITY

Self-love is just part of the solution. You also must believe in your ability to overcome the challenges in your life. Many of the challenges you will face as a young mother will have you questioning your ability to succeed. It's times like these that you will need to lean in and remember that you can get through it.

You will also understand why you are doing those things: your child. Your child is your "*why?*"; they are your source of strength to keep moving forward. You would do anything to provide your child with a better upbringing than you had, and you're going to use that strength to make sure you can overcome the challenges facing you as soon as possible. All it takes is believing in your ability to do just that. Never get discouraged or tell yourself that you can't overcome those obstacles.

CONTINUED PERSONAL DEVELOPMENT; NEVER STOP LEARNING

When I was growing up, everything was changing. Nothing stayed the way I wanted it to, and I knew I wouldn't have a say in how it changed. As I have grown older and continued to learn, I've realized that nothing stays the same in this life. This is why personal development is very important.

There will never be a point in life when you will have learned everything there is to know. You might have a fancy college degree, but that doesn't mean anything if you don't continue to educate yourself and learn more. It takes real-world experience and help from mentors, coaches, and support systems that have been where you've been. They can help you learn more than what is taught in the classroom.

I strongly believe you must always be open to personal development, because the truth is we don't know everything, even when we act like we do in order to impress others. We must continue to develop our minds. We want to be good role models for our children as they grow up and ask questions. We need to be the ones they are leaning on. We continue to educate ourselves so that we can teach them as well.

OVERCOMING OBSTACLES

Obstacles are a part of life which help us to continue developing ourselves. Everyone's story is different, but I can give you some tips on the things I had to overcome. These pointers will help you to remember that you're not alone. Overcoming your own difficulties can be done. I know from experience: I had to reevaluate everything that was going on in my life and make some tough decisions in order to overcome my obstacles.

I had relied heavily on my parents when I had my first child because I was so young, and they were all I had. I wanted to progress in life, and with their help I could do that. However, as I mentioned earlier, all the support I had in the beginning fell away when my dad left this earth, and my mom fell ill.

A lot of the decisions I had to make were extreme. This was an obstacle for me because it was something I wasn't used to. It was a huge reality check, and it made me realize that there were going to be many more challenges and bridges that I would have to cross. I had to make a lot of tough decisions and make plans to get through those obstacles.

What this means for you is that when you are faced with a challenge, muster up the strength to know that you can push through any storm. God will not leave you or give you more than you can bear. Keep *the light at the end of the tunnel* in mind as you enter the dark, treacherous moments along your journey.

MASTERING EFFECTIVE COMMUNICATION

Effective communication is another means to parent with confidence. You will need to effectively communicate with everyone around you. Whether it's to your child or to a doctor, school administrator or teacher, if you can't clearly communicate your thoughts and feelings, it will tear you down personally and can create a whole host of problems.

The ability to effectively communicate will give you even more confidence in yourself to address things in the proper manner and with self-assurance. You will be a resilient parent and stand up for your child, able to discipline them effectively and teach your child what they need to know as they grow older.

THE ART OF LISTENING

Listening is a very important part of effective communication. In fact, it is the most important communication skill. Listening is somewhat difficult for me because I consider myself to be a problem-solver. When I hear about a problem, I go into what I like to call "solution mode." I start to look for a solution before considering all the facts of the problem. While it's good to successfully and strategically come up with ways to resolve a situation, sometimes this mindset leads to missing a lot of the facts associated with the problem. I have learned to listen thoroughly so I can be an effective communicator.

As you learn how to effectively listen to what somebody else is saying, taking time to dissect everything they say, you will be able to let yourself think thoroughly before you respond. Communication is a great skill to impart to your child, and they will learn from your example as you focus on learning yourself. This will be very beneficial to you, as it is a skill you will both need now and until the end of your life.

THE POWER OF QUESTIONS

Asking questions is another part of communicating effectively. Questions can help us to develop ourselves further. Without the right questions, you will not get the answers you need. You should have confidence in what you want. Good communication is a skill, so when you are communicating, you're communicating with a purpose. If you know what questions to ask or what answers you want, you will have the upper hand: you'll be better prepared, have more clarity, and yield better results for any situation.

PICKING AND CHOOSING YOUR BATTLES

Some things are not worth fighting over. Now, that does not mean putting your values on the back burner to accommodate someone else. This means you're going to come up against situations where you will have to pick and choose what to fight for, especially if it's something you think is important enough for you to make a big deal out of.

For example: you get a rude call from your supervisor about a correction that is required on your work assignment. After further review, you find that your submission was indeed correct, and the supervisor was wrong. Some people would pick a battle about this situation, making the issue more than what it is worth. The responsible thing to do is kindly inform your supervisor of your findings and leave it there. Trust me; your supervisor will already feel like an idiot for the way he or she addressed the situation, so taking the mature route will give them a new level of respect for you as an employee.

When I say you should pick and choose your battles, all I'm saying is that there are going to be times when you will have to make decisions and ask questions such as: *Is this something I should make a big deal about? Or is this something that I can put off and make a note about should the same situation come up in the future?*

With that, I offer you some advice to parent and live your life with confidence. You must really dig deep into who you are and truly identify things that matter to you. Don't look at other people, at social media, at your friends, or at other influences. Make the decision based on what is important to you. Understand what is important to you as a person and identify the values you want to instill in your family. This will help you to always put your values first. You will succeed at anything you do because you are looking out for yourself and your family.

MY **STRATEGY #1** NOTES

What did you learn?

_____
_____
_____
_____
_____
_____

Write an affirmation that arose for you from this chapter.

_____
_____
_____

What steps will you take next?

_____
_____
_____
_____
_____
_____

MY **STRATEGY #1** NOTES

MY **STRATEGY #1** NOTES

MY **STRATEGY #1** NOTES

MY **STRATEGY #1** NOTES

MY **STRATEGY #1** NOTES

MY **STRATEGY #1** NOTES

SUCCESS STRATEGY #2

ACKNOWLEDGING YOUR NEW REALITY; MANAGING SUCCESS WHILE PARENTING

IDENTIFYING YOUR SUPPORT SYSTEM

In life, we go through many stages. Some of them are harder than others, and having a support system can go a long way. But how exactly do you identify that support system? How do you know who genuinely has your best interests at heart? There will be many people that play a role in your life, but that does not mean they will all be your biggest supporters. Someone who shows you time after time that they encourage your success and respect your decisions is usually your biggest supporter. Although initially it will be challenging, you must let them into your life and invite them into your personal space.

Remember; your most significant supporter is someone you can trust. You must allow them to impart little nuggets of advice and teach you lessons that are going to help you and your child. Understand that they want the best for you unless they show you otherwise. Trust the process.

Many of the young mothers I have worked with have been a bit wary of receiving input from others; however, to fully identify and utilize your support system, you must be open to receiving advice. It can come from anywhere: school, church, a neighbor, or a family member.

The support from these sources can go a long way, and is recognizable as you feel a shift in your daily actions and decision-making abilities. You'll have to be open, accepting, and trusting of your support network. If you believe that your supporters genuinely want you to succeed or help you and your child get into a better situation, then you are going to have to break down the barriers between yourself and the world.

In most cases, family and friends are the most significant supporters, but there are other means of support out there, too. Take advantage of any and all community resources available in your area. To learn more, contact your local social service department and non-profit research organizations. Google will be your best friend. Do not be afraid to get community help. Because this help is temporary, it is best to take as much of it as you can to help you and your child move forward in life.

SOCIAL CHANGE/BALANCE

Being a mother is rewarding, but parenting is not easy. It doesn't come with a handbook or a boatload of people reaching out to help you all the time. You don't have to be a mother 24/7—it's alright to have a social life! However, you must find a way to balance "me" time with your regular life responsibilities. You want to be able to enjoy time with your friends and still be a highly effective parent at the same time.

It's important to have some friends who share your values. Of course you're going to have friends who don't think exactly like you do, but that's okay, too: no one is going to be just like you, because you are unique. You want to find a circle of friends that can complement where you want to go in life. It won't be easy, and it will take time to find that circle of friends, but it's mandatory.

Now, you might already have friends in your life, and that's fine; however, when you want more in life, you must shift your circle to include people who want to see you grow, including the people that you are learning from. It's not going to happen overnight but trust me: as your mindset begins to shift, so will your friends list. As you grow, you will continue to evaluate your time and who you're spending it with. I am not saying you can't keep your sandbox friends. This is just a heads-up that change is coming.

In a nutshell, evaluate your friends, looking for those that want to see you grow and can help you grow as a person. You can't just let them help you to grow; you must provide value in the friendship as well. After all, birds of a feather flock together.

I recommend that you surround yourself with friends who will watch your back and help you gain the knowledge you need to succeed in life. If you're the one who is helping or you find yourself giving your friends all the answers without being able to lean on them, then that is a sign you need to find a new crowd who can provide you with the support your old set of friends could not.

Overall, when you're working, parenting, and trying to balance your social life, things become very demanding. Your choices are very slim and should be considered wisely. It is critical to establish a routine in your household to allow some mommy time.

BUILDING MEANINGFUL RELATIONSHIPS

In life it is best to create as many meaningful relationships as possible, where you and the other person both benefit from it. A meaningful relationship is not just with your friends; it is with the support systems you have already identified.

A meaningful relationship is one that fosters a connection that can potentially help you in the long run, while also being a benefit to the other person. You do not want to be the one to continually take without giving anything back. You want to be one who adds value to a relationship. If the relationship has a lot of negative energy, then you do not need to be in it. You must seek positive relationships that will help you to grow as a person.

You should look for someone with shared goals, such as wanting to pursue an education. Say you're employed but want to go back to school, and you have a friend who is a parent like you and also works and goes to school. You may want to reach out to this person who is where you want to be in your life so they can motivate you. Look for some positive actions that they are taking, and let them know that what they are doing is something you are interested in as well.

Sometimes you must let go of people you've always been around and introduce yourself to new people in order to be able to grow. It's part of the process of becoming a better person, and the only way you are going to identify people who are positive influences is by understanding where you want to be. Once you know where you want to be in life, the kinds of relationships you seek out will change. You will know instantly those not meant to be in your life, those who you should move further and further away from.

IDENTIFYING WHAT IS IMPORTANT AND WHY?

To be successful as a parent and in life, you must understand your *why*. To be successful as a parent, your *why* is your child, but to be successful as a person, understanding your *why* and the reason for what you are doing now in your life will be the vehicle to your success.

At this point in your life, your child is your *why*. For me, my child was my *why*. As a parent, creating a legacy and some generational wealth is why I'm doing what I am doing today. Growing up as a young parent and not having all the resources that I am providing to you today is what inspired me to write this book.

There is always going to be a *why* which will be the vehicle that drives you where you need to go in life. And once you understand that *why* and can piece those things together, nothing will stop you from doing the things you want to do.

Knowing your *why* is not the only thing you need in order to be successful in life. You must also try to identify your purpose as well. Even I still struggle with this. To me, identifying purpose is about recognizing what I am destined to do in my life. Discover what you are passionate about and what brings you joy, and it will come easily to you. You will feel it and when you do, you'll think: *Wow, this is what I am destined to do. This is my purpose in life. This what I want to do.*

It's a process that is going to gradually happen as you continue to grow as a person. As you continue to mature and experience life, you will be able to more easily identify your purpose. It is something you will have to meditate on. When you are able to listen to the voice coming from deep down inside, then you will feel it instantly.

Your purpose in life will come to you when you least expect it. You could be at home relaxing or meditating. You never know what will prompt you to discover your purpose. You might find your purpose while working or while spending time outdoors with your child. It all depends on what is happening in your life and what you discover inside yourself.

Never let someone else decide your purpose in life. You must decide on your own, and your support system will be with you along the way. Just trust yourself and listen to the advice of your support system, and you will do fine.

MY **STRATEGY #2** NOTES

What did you learn?

_____
_____
_____
_____
_____
_____

Write an affirmation that arose for you from this chapter.

_____
_____
_____

What steps will you take next?

_____
_____
_____
_____
_____
_____

MY **STRATEGY #2** NOTES

MY **STRATEGY #2** NOTES

MY **STRATEGY #2** NOTES

MY **STRATEGY #2** NOTES

MY **STRATEGY #2** NOTES

MY **STRATEGY #2** NOTES

SUCCESS STRATEGY #3

WORK/LIFE BALANCE

FORMING A ROUTINE

Life can be hectic, but we must find strategies to balance how we spend our time. At the end of the day we have the ultimate control over how organized and balanced our lives are. To some, it may seem like they do not always have that much control because employers, children, and other family members can be very demanding. However, to maintain our sanity, we must take control and create this balanced life.

The best way to balance your life is to plan everything out. This all starts with organization. You need to have some type of system that sets aside time to tend to various responsibilities, as well as some "me" time. Obviously, it also has to be flexible, because even the best-laid plans won't always work out as anticipated. Life is full of curve balls and surprises. However, having a schedule or a plan will eliminate a lot of chaos, allowing you to function better at home, work, school—wherever. Knowing in advance what needs to be done, when it needs to be done, and how it needs to be done will actually save time and reduce stress. To achieve this, you'll need to be open to delegation, asking for help, and being flexible. Don't freak out if plans need to be adjusted. Not every situation that arises will be flexible—and not every person you deal with will be flexible, either—so you must be flexible and adjust your plans accordingly.

That is why you must have an emergency contact, someone you can always reach out to who can help you out when situations come up that you need help with. Perhaps your boss gives you a last-minute project that will keep you late at work. Having a friend you can call to pick up your kids from school allows you to finish your work while making sure your kids are looked after. Arranging for "Plan B" in advance will simplify your life and prevent undue stress. Just having that balance and being a little more organized while making sure that you can leave some gaps for the unexpected will make life easier.

ADEQUATE FAMILY TIME

Finding time for family is crucial, but many of us do not spend as much time together as we would like to. Family is the key to both our kids' well-being and our own. No matter if you are married or a single young mother, your kids need to spend family time with you—and you benefit from it just as much as they do.

Your kids need to have the time to enjoy your company, to laugh and joke together, and to develop important memories about the things you do with each other, even if it's just eating meals together at the table or scheduling a weekly movie night. These are the things that they look forward to. Just creating these memories is critical to building a strong family because you will always have those times to look back on when times get hard.

BE YOUR CHILD'S BIGGEST SUPPORTER

Your child needs you to be their biggest supporter. They need an unconditional cheerleader in their life, and you as the parent—as a mom—will be that supporter, helping them to navigate through both the good times and the challenging times. You should be the one rooting for them when something goes great in their life, such as when they make their school's sports teams or get cast in the school play. You need to share their excitement when they learn something new and exciting. You need to offer encouragement when they face challenges.

When you show them that support, you show them how much you love them. As they grow older, it helps them develop self-esteem, which is a crucial element in achieving success of any kind and avoiding the many pitfalls that will trip them up. When we are always there for them, rooting for them to succeed, it lets them know that we care about their accomplishments and that we will be there when they fail.

You should be your child's biggest supporter because you need them to be able to look up to you and be trusting enough to talk to you when something is not going right in their life. They should be able to tell you anything and just know that you will be there for them every step of the way.

THE VALUE OF RESPECT

Respect is a two-way street. We not only need to earn and expect respect from our children, but we also need to respect them in turn: treat people the way that you want to be treated. Though our children may be young, they need us to see them as individuals who deserve our respect. As they grow older, we can request the same respect that we have shown them.

This is a powerful part of work and life balance. Children who are taught the value of respecting others' needs will grow into adults who are able to respect what you are doing as an individual and a mom—and vice versa. No matter the situation, whether it's in the workplace or at home, we must maintain a level of respect that we show others and that we request for ourselves.

BE A GOOD EXAMPLE

We must always set a good example for our children. They learn more by watching us than being told, and we must show them the right way to act around others and family members. However, there will be times where we will have trouble setting a good example.

We are all human, and we will make mistakes. We are not perfect individuals and neither are our children. We should understand that and know how to deal with the things that life throws at us because the way we deal with these things can have a lasting impact on our children.

When you have low self-esteem or talk derisively about the world around you, then your child will see that and act that way toward themselves. Being able to identify those issues is the first step in changing your behavior. It is challenging but necessary to work on these things. That means you should dig deep and focus on your personal development. Knowing that your positivity rubs off on your kids should inspire you to keep at it.

Our kids are sponges and will absorb negative energy if we continue to radiate it. If that happens, then they may in turn spread negativity to the people they know, or grow up with low self-esteem as well.

BECOME THE INFLUENCER FOR YOUR FAMILY

Every day, we are influenced by things we see on television that entice us—cars to buy, food to eat, gadgets to play with, and other things we really don't need. We should be the ones who influence our children as much as possible.

What we do and what we eat are just a couple of things that can influence our children. If you want to incorporate exercise into their routine, you must exercise. If you want them to eat more vegetables, then you need to make more vegetables. If you want them to have a healthy body image, you need to stop fretting over your looks or dress size.

Kids watch us to see what is okay for them to eat and do. You need to be the one who sets that tone in your house so you can influence some of the things that they do. If you eat fast food every day or eat out almost every night, then your child will believe that it is alright, and they won't learn about proper nutrition or the fun of cooking a meal from scratch. You have to start setting examples and embracing your role as the influencer in your household, making the decisions that you want your children to adopt as they get older.

MY **STRATEGY #3** NOTES

What did you learn?

_____
_____
_____
_____
_____

Write an affirmation that arose for you from this chapter.

_____
_____
_____

What steps will you take next?

_____
_____
_____
_____
_____
_____

MY **STRATEGY #3** NOTES

MY **STRATEGY #3** NOTES

MY **STRATEGY #3** NOTES

MY **STRATEGY #3** NOTES

MY **STRATEGY #3** NOTES

MY **STRATEGY #3** NOTES

SUCCESS STRATEGY #4

MANAGING YOUR MONEY; BUDGETING, SAVING, *NEED* VS. *WANT*

They say that money makes the world go 'round, but how do we prevent it from controlling us? We start by budgeting how and when we spend our money. We must also start saving what money we can for emergencies.

If you want to purchase a home or a car, you must create a budget and begin saving up for those big purchases. The same is also true for smaller items. The point is, you must always make sure that you are putting some amount of money away, even if it's just five or ten dollars a week. Always put something away for a rainy day.

SIMPLE CREDIT

Simple credit is just that: simple. It is mostly about credit scores. You must know about the three credit bureaus and how to get in touch with them. Identity theft is a major problem when dealing with credit. There are many companies that claim to help prevent your identity from being stolen, but it is up to you to decide which one to go with.

Your credit score can help you when buying a car or a house. Having good credit makes it easy to buy those things, but if your credit score is not the best, then it is harder to buy those things. You will be charged higher interest rates because the lender will view you as a greater risk. Learning your credit score will go a long way to help you manage your money. There are several ways to get a copy of your credit reports, such as www.creditkarma.com and www.credit.com/free-credit-score. Also, credit unions and banks will sometimes provide this information as an account holder's perk.

Below is contact information for the three main credit bureaus:

Equifax
P.O. Box 740241
Atlanta, GA 30374-0241
800-685-1111
www.equifax.com.

Experian
P.O. Box 2104
Allen, TX 75013-0949
888-EXPERIAN (397-3742)
www.experian.com.

TransUnion
P.O. Box 1000
Chester, PA 19022
800-916-8800
www.transunion.com.

Annual Credit Report
https://www.annualcreditreport.com/

INCOME

Your income is a big factor in determining how you will manage your money. Based on your personality or work history, you may fall into one of the following categories:

- Employee: A person hired by another person or a company to perform a specific role, service or pre-defined set of responsibilities. Examples include government workers, Metro staff, etc.
- Self-Employed: A person who earns money working for themselves. Examples include freelancers, consultants, and those who organize their own work and tax payments without a boss' oversight.
- Entrepreneur: A person who starts their own business. It can be as small as a local bicycle repair shop or as big as Facebook.
- Investor: A person or organization that puts money into financial sectors, property, etc. with the expectation of achieving a profit.

When I was growing as a young mother, I did not have these options outlined for me. It was never framed as a choice or broken down into these categories.

I had to support my household, so I had to have an income, but as I've shown, there are plenty of options for how to earn money. As you continue to develop as an individual, you will figure out which type of work you are best suited for. Managing your money early on and understanding your options gives you the advantage to create the life of your dreams.

Most of us were brought up to think that we cannot be successful at owning our own companies; that the American way is to go to school and get a good job. Things are changing, and to your advantage. You have more control now than ever before to create your own reality and your dream job.

MY **STRATEGY #4** NOTES

What did you learn?

_____
_____
_____
_____
_____
_____

Write an affirmation that arose for you from this chapter.

_____
_____
_____

What steps will you take next?

_____
_____
_____
_____
_____
_____

MY **STRATEGY #4** NOTES

MY **STRATEGY #4** NOTES

MY **STRATEGY #4** NOTES

MY **STRATEGY #4** NOTES

MY **STRATEGY #4** NOTES

MY **STRATEGY #4** NOTES

SUCCESS STRATEGY #5

SHIFTING FROM THE *I* MINDSET

As a parent you're no longer just responsible for yourself. You can't have an *I* mindset. Total selfishness can't exist because it isn't just about you anymore. The *I* mindset must shift to *we*. Here are some of the decisions you are making every day that are now affecting your child:

How will creating a budget affect my child?
How do my values affect my child?
How does this new relationship affect my child?

So many of your life decisions must have your children's best interests in mind. You are their provider and protector. You will have to establish a college fund for them, and this might require some sacrifices, which could mean not getting your nails done every two weeks. You will have to pay for school clothes, field trips, and provide lunch money. There is sacrifice involved. Seeking your own desires isn't always practical in a parenting relationship.

EFFECTIVE DECISION MAKING

When making decisions, you want to ensure they are the right ones for your family. This may mean doing some research, because making emotionally impulsive decisions tends to hinder one's success. It is important that all decisions are thought out. Remember: your decisions affect more than just your life. You can't say: *It's only me. I can move into this neighborhood because I'm comfortable with this.* You have to think about the schools in the neighborhood and its safety. There are a lot of different things that you're going to have to take into consideration when you're making decisions. Research is key. What is best for your child should always be the main focus.

SUCCESS MINDSET: THE POWER OF POSITIVE THOUGHTS

Having positive thoughts is crucial because it determines your life's outcome. Negative thoughts breed negative spaces. Positivity breeds optimism. It is hard to have faith and see the good in life when you are constantly thinking or speaking negatively. You live what you speak. It becomes your reality. It's been proven scientifically that when you think positively, that energy flows out into the world. In order to be successful, you must breathe it, think it, and see it! Your actions will soon follow.

Negative thinking will not move you in the right direction. It will keep you stagnant. Negative thoughts weigh you down. Negative mindsets also isolate you. Most individuals love being around people who exude positive energy. People know who you are from the moment you walk into a room. When entering a room, you should be so positive that the negative energy in the room is forced to shift.

Get in the habit of training your mind to think positively. It is important that you teach your children this skill as well. When a negative thought enters, replace it with a positive one. Put this into practice daily. Remember: we actually become what we think.

We can holistically co-create our success just by adjusting our thought process. It's called the Law of Attraction, and it has been proven to work.

If you think positive thoughts, then you will attract positive things into your life. Positive people can attract money and success. You can obtain success as a parent based on what you tell yourself and how you think about your parenting skills. You must tell yourself: *I'm a good mom, it's okay. My kids are going to be just fine,* instead of saying: *Oh my gosh, I'm so worried about my kids. They're going to be criminals. I'm doing this by myself; I don't have any support.*

BREAK THROUGH MENTAL BLOCKS

While we know intellectually that anything is possible if we set our minds to it, we often hold ourselves back subconsciously. Until we break through the mental blocks that keep us playing small, we will never realize our capabilities.

What causes mental blockage? Fear. Naysayers. Having people who fill your head with self-doubt. Not believing in your own abilities. Thinking that you aren't worthy or equipped enough. All these things can cause mental blocks. Over the years, our life stories have revealed things that cause us to fear. Our childhoods and life experiences have programmed us in positive as well as negative ways. In order to get past these blockages, we must unlearn and deprogram what is causing us to remain in chains.

One of the ways we can do this is to create our own realities. We can't look at what our parents taught us. We can't look at our childhood environments and our pasts. Our minds must be on our futures and what is best for us *now*. Release yourself from the past. Stop looking backward. Learn from it and take what will be beneficial to you in the future. Create new stories that you can take with you and pass on to others.

Your dreams are too big for you to keep playing small. It is time to take action, and time to stop doubting your abilities. Things don't have to be perfect. Focus on progress, not perfection. I have learned to take baby steps. Forward movement is better than no movement at all.

It is okay to stretch yourself and move out of your comfort zone. When you believe in yourself, you invest in yourself. You refuse to play small. That is how dreams become realities. It all happens outside of your comfort zone.

When I was a young adult, reading was a big part of my learning style. My mom wasn't able to teach me a lot about being a responsible young woman because she couldn't explain to me what was never explained to her. I realized at a very young age that survival was one of the only lessons taught in urban communities. I started reading books and teaching myself through stories how to rise above my environment. While reading these stories, I decided that one day I would write a book, although it took me a number of years to finally do it.

One day I attended an event that offered me the opportunity to become a co-author of an anthology called *Artificial Beauté, the Breakthrough: Six Stories of Transforming from Hurt to Healing*. I thought really hard about it and decided to get my feet wet. This experience offered me the chance to help others through storytelling. My personal quest for knowledge has continued to inspire me to write books with hopes of helping millions of readers.

Allow yourself some quiet time to reflect; journal and focus on what's positive instead of negative. As moms, we sometimes tend to think too hard, which can cause negativity to seep into our minds. We may not have all of the answers, and that is okay.

Taking time to pray has also helped me tremendously. Whenever I'm going through anything that's really bothering me, I instantly say a prayer. After praying, I feel like the world is lifted off my shoulders. Life happens. When it becomes cloudy and gray, you must have a strategy that will help redirect your focus from the roadblocks back to purpose and promise. Prayer has helped me get there. I allow God to help me release the things that are out of my control, because so many things are out of our control. I give it to Him, and He helps me deal with the problems I face. I have faith that He will take care of it.

CRUSHING LIMITING BELIEFS

There is so much hype about being more productive, eliminating distractions, and prioritizing. While these things are important, if you don't first start with crushing your limiting beliefs, you'll find yourself struggling and working harder than you need to. When you envision success in your mind, it creates an energetic flow that attracts all the resources you need to make it happen.

When you control your thoughts and believe that you can make something happen, it gives you the energy to know that you can knock down all of those limited beliefs. There will always be something that will make you feel as if you are being held back. You're going to feel like there's something that you don't have. You will strive for perfection instead of progress. The reality is that we're never going to be perfect. You will have to remind yourself of this daily. Learn to control your thoughts. Knock down anything negative that may keep you from reaching your success. You can and will win as long as you keep your eyes on the goal.

Think about a time in your life where you told yourself you couldn't do it, and then think about a time in your life where you stretched yourself. Maybe you were afraid to ask for a promotion at work. Maybe you were afraid to let that guy know you were interested in him, but when you did, it all worked out. You took the necessary steps. You came up with a plan of action. This begins with getting it out of your head and putting it down on paper.

Scripture tells us to *write the vision and to make it plain*. Successful businesses form when a business plan is written. We must write what we desire in life.

I remember a time where I had to crush my limiting beliefs and choose *me*. After having applied for a promotion at my job, my director was walking around looking for me. I went to his office thinking I got the job. When I walked in, he told me that I wasn't on the list. Though I wasn't on the list, my director stated that I did interview well. He also wanted me to explain why he should give me the job. I was extremely nervous and filled with a myriad of emotions, yet I had to put all of that aside. And it was difficult to do. First, I started to doubt myself and my abilities. But I couldn't stay there. I looked at my director and told him why I was the perfect candidate for the position. Standing up for myself, I identified my abilities, my worth, and why I was an asset to the organization. When I walked out of my director's office, I left with the promotion. I was able to just crush all those negative thoughts that started going through my mind.

Think about a time where you told yourself no and a time where you stretched yourself. How do these two instances differ? Think about what happened when you stretched past your fears and said yes to yourself. If you want to, write about that experience below:

___

___

___

___

___

___

UP-LEVEL YOUR BELIEFS

Strive to be the best version of yourself, and believe it's possible. Living life in abundance means that you are focused on the quality of everything you do and experience.

As you continue to grow, there will be times that you have to push yourself to up-level. It is like walking up a staircase. With each level of growth, you move to the next stop. There will be times that you may slip, fall, and get knocked down a step, but you can always get back up, learn from the situation, and up-level again. Eventually, you will realize that the sky is the limit. With personal growth, there are new levels and dimensions to explore in every area of your life.

For every area of your life—career, financial, spiritual, physical, intellectual, family, social, etc.—assess and write out your satisfaction level on a scale from one to ten, with ten being the most satisfied. Circle the three areas with the least satisfaction. Then, ask yourself what you could do to make it a ten. You will dive more into this activity in Strategy #6.

MY **STRATEGY #5** NOTES

What did you learn?

_____
_____
_____
_____
_____
_____

Write an affirmation that arose for you from this chapter.

_____
_____
_____

What steps will you take next?

_____
_____
_____
_____
_____
_____

MY **STRATEGY #5** NOTES

MY **STRATEGY #5** NOTES

MY **STRATEGY #5** NOTES

MY **STRATEGY #5** NOTES

MY **STRATEGY #5** NOTES

MY **STRATEGY #5** NOTES

SUCCESS STRATEGY #6

SELF-REFLECTION

Women who exude confidence and are able to affect change are very clear on who they are and what they want. Evaluate your current life to determine what is stopping you from up-leveling. Who is holding you back from living your best life? Sometimes, up-leveling your life means leaving people behind.

Literally look in the mirror and ask yourself these questions:

Who am I?
What do I want?
What do I need to let go of in my current life to get the life I want?
What am I willing to sacrifice?
What does the best me look like?

Reflecting on these questions regularly will change the way you think, feel, and act for the better.

Everything that will help you up-level is already within you. When you take the time to ask yourself reflective questions, focus initially on qualities within you, your habits, your strengths, and building around them.

You are in control and can make the necessary changes. Ask yourself if there are any bad habits that you want to let go of: being impatient? The tendency to quickly make assumptions and jump to conclusions? Laziness? If so, make some changes.

SELF-PERCEPTION

Perception is an internal process. What do you want to invite into your life? How do you perceive your quality of life?

Many women perceive more money, the right partner, a nice car, etc., as steps to success. There is nothing wrong with that in itself, but you should start by reviewing what kinds of things you want to invite into your life. Better health? Acceptance? Confidence? Being kind to yourself and others? Identifying habits that will enrich your life?

Want to feel loved more? Then love more. Remember that love is something that needs to be expressed. What you give is what you receive.

The more beautiful your inner world becomes, the more beauty the outer world will reflect back to you. The bridge between both is your perception and the actions you take.

MY **STRATEGY #6** NOTES

What did you learn?

_____
_____
_____
_____
_____

Write an affirmation that arose for you from this chapter.

_____
_____
_____

What steps will you take next?

_____
_____
_____
_____
_____

MY **STRATEGY #6** NOTES

MY **STRATEGY #6** NOTES

MY **STRATEGY #6** NOTES

MY **STRATEGY #6** NOTES

MY **STRATEGY #6** NOTES

MY **STRATEGY #6** NOTES

MY **STRATEGY #6** NOTES

SUCCESS STRATEGY #7

CREATING A DREAM BOARD

A goal without a deadline is just a dream.
— Robert Herjavec

Merriam-Webster defines a dream as a strongly desired goal or purpose. When you were younger, you may have had a dream of becoming a doctor, a lawyer, or a teacher. Many of your dreams back then may have been based on your surroundings, books, television, or your favorite person. As you have matured and figured out who you are, your childhood dreams may have changed.

To dream is to be able to visualize where you want to go in life. A dreamer has a vision. They can see it clearly. There aren't any limits, and they strive daily to reach the kind of life they envision. When one truly understands their purpose and grabs onto their dream, they refuse to allow life's circumstances to interfere with accomplishing it.

Dreaming requires not giving up. When I dream, I don't see any limits on the outcomes of my life. All I can see are the possibilities and the opportunities. I have been successful because I see where I want to be, and I have taken the necessary steps to get there. I believed in myself, and I knew that I deserved the life that I envisioned. It wasn't easy, but because I understood my worth and my *why*, I was able to move forward.

What would have happened if I had only been a dreamer and never an executor? Yes, dreaming is important, but I needed to do more than dream. Those dreams had to come out of my head, and I had to develop a plan to ensure manifestation occurred.

Creating a dream board is an effective way to ensure that your dreams become a reality. Dream boards allow us to create spaces where we see the things we want to accomplish before they actually happen. We are visual creatures, and when we visualize doing something, our brains respond as if we are really doing it. For example, if you imagine doing a free throw, the chemicals produced in your brain and the electrical impulses sent to the muscles are identical to those that will be sent if you were actually doing it.

Your brain doesn't always know the difference between what's real and what's imaginary. This is why visualization is a useful tool for achieving a goal. By seeing yourself accomplishing it, you're training your mind and body for the real thing. The more vividly and frequently you visualize your goal and activate your senses with all the details and emotions, the more likely you are to achieve it.

My mission is to encourage you to dream bigger and write down your vision. This is why it is so important for me to offer the workshops that I hold. My classes teach necessary subjects such as leadership, financial literacy, bridging success, and lifestyle transformation. I motivate and inspire teenage and young mothers to live intentionally and to never give up despite their challenging circumstances. My goal is to help you break through barriers of your past and identify your full potential so I can lead you on the path to meaningful employment, personal development, and financial independence.

Executing my dreams and reaching goals to help others also allows me to create a legacy for my family, as it can for you and your family. Witnessing me carrying out my mission to support other young moms enables my children to see the benefits of pursuing their dreams and living in their purpose. My accomplishments are providing generational wealth and dignity for my children, my grandchildren, and the young moms I help around the world.

WHAT EXACTLY IS A DREAM BOARD?

The most basic definition of a dream board is a group of images, quotes, and symbols that have significant meaning to you. They represent your dream life.

Motivational messages, inspiring quotes—anything that makes you smile or brightens your day is a good fit for your dream board. Your dream board might include things you see posted on social media, phrases you read and write down in your journal, or even sweet things others have said about you.

Creating a dream board can be as simple as cutting photos, words, quotes, and passages out of a magazine and pasting them on a poster board, or even just tacking them up on your bedroom wall. It can be as fun as a dream board party with friends. Your creative options are endless.

You can always join my Facebook group and participate in our virtual dream board parties or register for our live events. Each year, I host an annual Speak Life Vision Board Paint Party Tour, which is similar to a dream board party. This annual event is geared towards moms and women in business, or anyone who is looking to take their lives to the next level. It's a day full of creative learning, networking, goal-setting, building vision/dream boards, painting, and enjoying good laughs with like-minded women.

We've even decided to host a tour for young children featuring youth entrepreneurs and youth service providers. Stay connected and join in the fun!

You can get a free copy of my *Dream Board Guide*.

It is easy to plan out your dreams when you have a personal mission statement for your life. Why are you here? What have you been called to accomplish? How will accomplishing your dreams change the lives of others? These questions can help guide you. Your personal mission statement, when identified, will set the tone for how you live your life. Knowing your personal mission statement will help you to choose who should and shouldn't be in your life. It will help you decide what you should and shouldn't do daily. Every action and step that you make should push you toward your personal mission statement. It is easier to create your dream board once you have established it.

There isn't a right or wrong way to create a dream board. They are individual projects. They are personal. You can make a yearly or even a five-year dream board. Once you have made a decision, *dream big*. Think about your short- and long-term goals, and place them on your board. What are some phrases that motivate you? Place them on your board. What are your deepest desires for your life? Place them on your board. Remember: the goal is to get it out of your head and in front of your eyes.

MY **STRATEGY #7** NOTES

What did you learn?

_____
_____
_____
_____
_____

Write an affirmation that arose for you from this chapter.

_____
_____
_____

What steps will you take next?

_____
_____
_____
_____
_____
_____

MY **STRATEGY #7** NOTES

MY **STRATEGY #7** NOTES

MY **STRATEGY #7** NOTES

MY **STRATEGY #7** NOTES

MY **STRATEGY #7** NOTES

MY **STRATEGY #7** NOTES

MY **STRATEGY #7** NOTES

SUCCESS STRATEGY #8

CREATING YOUR ACTION PLAN FOR SUCCESS

You've got to know what you want. This is central to acting on your intentions. When you know what you want, you realize that all there is left then is time management. You'll manage your time to achieve your goals because you clearly know what you're trying to achieve in your life.

— Hunter "Patch" Adams

I live intentionally. Setting an intention has improved my life. An intention is defined as a determination to act in a certain way. When I was a young teen mom, I had to be more intentional about my decision making. Once I became a parent, I had trouble understanding that I couldn't be selfish. Before I had children, my focus had been on what was best for me. It was simple living: my main goal was ensuring that I was happy and taken care of. I was used to not having responsibilities. When my first child was born, things changed. My mindset had to shift, and I had to focus on what was best for my child.

In the beginning, I was still trying to work and attend school full-time. I was forced to make some changes and live my life in a way that intentionally blessed my child and me. I had to knock down some doors. School was one of them.

Setting an intention should occur as soon as you find yourself having to make adult decisions. Once you transition into adulthood and parenthood, all decisions should be intentional. Living life recklessly and ignorantly isn't an option. The decisions you make now affect more than yourself. Decisions should be thought out. They should be purpose-driven. They should redirect you back to your personal mission statement.

SET INTENTIONS AND TAKE INSPIRED ACTION.

Identifying an action plan will ensure your success.

Every day begins with a plan. Each time we open our eyes is a gift. It is imperative that you cherish your gift and use your time wisely. It is easy to miss opportunities when your intentions are not set. It is easy to lose motivation and momentum without a plan.

Ask your higher self to show you what's truly important to accomplish today. I have often said this prayer: *Dear God, you are the master planner. Show me what is important for me to accomplish today. Show me the steps to carry out my purpose and mission.*

When you ask for guidance, keep your eyes open for signs, nudges, and ideas that pop into your head. When you ask with a sincere heart, you can get direction on demand for the next steps. Make time to listen. Relax in a bath, sit in stillness, spend time in nature, or take a walk. The guidance will come. When the guidance arrives, you will be willing and ready to put in the work if you understand your *why*.

IDENTIFYING YOUR *WHY*

We all have reasons why we do certain things, why we make certain moves, choices, etc. Though our reasons may differ, our *why* is what fuels us to continue moving forward. My *why* is to break a generational curse. My *why* is to create a legacy for my children. Because of this, I have written this book, started my business, and continue to live intentionally. I will create a legacy and build generational wealth for my family. What is fueling you? Your *why* must be so huge that no one and nothing can deter you. Your *why* will be your backbone. It will keep you focused when distractions and negativity attempt to stop you.

There will be obstacles that will try to halt your progress. That is life. Unexpected situations occur. Things will happen that are out of your control. You may even feel like giving up at times. But when you think about your *why*, all the obstacles seem small and cease to appear in comparison to it. There is *nothing* that can stop a woman who is focused on her purpose. Come hell or high water, she will do all that she can to ensure that it comes to pass.

Why must you accomplish your dreams? What drives you? Identify your *why* below.

_____

_____

_____

_____

_____

_____

_____

_____

DREAMS + ACTION = PROGRESS

Dreams without actions are only blurred visions.

Faith without works is dead, meaning that if you have a dream, but you are not taking action, you won't see your dream become a reality. Your dreams and visions will not materialize without hard work. After time, they become blurry because you've lost focus and passion. The more action you take, the closer you will be to accomplishing your goals, and the closer you will be to seeing your dreams come to life. Without action, you will not see the progress and the dreams that you visualized and placed on your dream board.

What causes one to dream and not act? Fear. Lack of confidence. An inability to see past today.

You are called to do amazing things. These dreams aren't just for you. There is someone waiting for you to see the picture clearly and get to work. When your dreams become realities, they too can walk in their purpose.

What steps do you need to take to ensure that your dreams come to life? Identify them here.

_____

_____

_____

_____

_____

_____

_____

PRIORITIZING ACTIVITY: WHAT'S MOST IMPORTANT IN THIS STAGE OF LIFE?

Once you've identified what's most important to you and your family, you must then prioritize your actions. Don't compare your priorities to anyone else's. Remember: your priorities are dependent on your goals and dreams. For example, if you know that you want to save $1,000, then you know that you have to prioritize certain actions to help you accomplish that goal.

Goals differ based on the individual and the set of circumstances. First, identify where you are in life and where you want to go. Then prioritize the intentional behaviors and actions you can take to get there. Finally, remember your personal mission statement and your *why*, and do what is necessary to obtain the life you desire.

MY **STRATEGY #8** NOTES

What did you learn?

_____
_____
_____
_____
_____
_____

Write an affirmation that arose for you from this chapter.

_____
_____
_____

What steps will you take next?

_____
_____
_____
_____
_____
_____

MY **STRATEGY #8** NOTES

MY **STRATEGY #8** NOTES

MY **STRATEGY #8** NOTES

MY **STRATEGY #8** NOTES

MY **STRATEGY #8** NOTES

MY **STRATEGY #8** NOTES

SUCCESS STRATEGY #9

STEPS TO EXECUTING YOUR PLAN

> *Vision without action is a daydream. Action without vision is a nightmare.*
>
> — Japanese Proverb

Now that we have identified where you are and what you want to do, what's next? This section will help you gain clarity to be able to effectively create your dream life.

MEASURING FOR SUCCESS

Measuring for success starts with understanding your current position and establishing your definition of success. Everyone's definition of success is different. What does success look and feel like to you? Is it based on financial gains? Social status? Having that corner office? Once you have your definition, then you can measure the steps needed to get there.

Make sure that your definition is clear. This falls right in line with prioritizing your action steps towards success. It is imperative that you keep your personal mission statement, your *why*, and your priorities at the forefront of your mind at all times. This ensures that all of the goals you set will be successfully met.

SMALL STEPS = PROGRESS

You will never know what you can accomplish if you never start. Remember that as long as you are moving, you are making progress. All steps are created equal. Make a daily decision to go further than you did the day before. Each day that you move forward brings you closer to your goal. Focus on progress and not perfection. A woman with a plan wins as long as she doesn't stop moving.

NEVER GIVE UP

Giving up is not an option. The reality is that there will always be some roadblocks. There are going to be times when you feel lost, stuck, and uncertain. Things are going to fall apart, and it may seem as if nothing is working in your favor. Life is hard! You must make the decision *now* to never give up, because never giving up guarantees that you will continue to make progress. Struggle forward! Each step moves you towards your goal. Each step brings you closer to living your dream life.

DON'T BEAT YOURSELF UP; AWARD YOURSELF

If you set a goal and you don't reach that goal, it's not over. Reflect on what worked, what didn't, and how you can move to the next step. If you set a goal to lose weight or save money and something interferes with that goal, don't beat yourself up about it. Keep moving forward, refusing to give up.

When you accomplish those small and big goals, reward yourself. You deserve it. Do something nice for yourself. What makes you feel special? Do that thing. You want to reward yourself in a way that will push you to keep going even harder in the future.

Always—and I mean *always*—create a plan that is actionable. Act on your insights.

Every plan has to be actionable. A plan without action isn't a plan at all. Remember that your actions are connected to your vision. The vision and dream boards help push you because they provide visual stimulation. Use these visuals to help you take steps towards accomplishing the life you want to live.

Be persistent in finding ways on how you can practically follow up on your action steps.

Be clear.

WORK WITH A COACH OR MENTOR

Working with a coach will help you go farther and faster, with less effort. It will force you to spend regularly committed time working on your own business or career development activities. Find someone you look up to and respect. Look for someone you feel a connection to who is in alignment with your beliefs. Join an accountability group. Surround yourself with like-minded individuals. Taking these steps can help you upgrade your mindset, set goals, prioritize, brainstorm, and hold yourself accountable to getting it done.

Google is your best friend if you are having a hard time finding resources such as coaches, mentors, and more. Utilize social media to your advantage. Social media is not just a tool that allows you to meet friends; there are numerous benefits and resources available to social media users. There are many different free groups on a variety of platforms where you can get valuable information.

My Facebook group, called Mom N' Powerment, is free and filled with valuable information. It's full of like-minded women who are working toward the same goal. Seek out school counselors and community groups. There will be times when you must invest in yourself in order to obtain the knowledge that will propel you towards your next level. Find what works for your budget.

Just remember that the resources needed for you to be great are out there.

The reason I wrote this book was that I was a young mom with high expectations for life. I refused to allow my teen pregnancy to stop my dreams from becoming a reality for my child and me. Yes, I had to make tough decisions. Yes, I had to reevaluate some of the things that I did. No, I wasn't able to accomplish some of the goals in as timely a fashion as I would have wanted to.

But I didn't stop.

So remember this: you are not alone! Women are getting things done, no matter what. And you can too. Remember your *why*, prioritize, and take the necessary steps to create the life you want for you and your child.

Never stop believing in your vision. Download some free activity sheets and resources at:

https://www.momnpowerment.com/iymv_resources/

> *Never look back unless you are planning to go that way.*
> — Henry David Thoreau

MY **STRATEGY #9** NOTES

What did you learn?

_____
_____
_____
_____
_____
_____

Write an affirmation that arose for you from this chapter.

_____
_____
_____

What steps will you take next?

_____
_____
_____
_____
_____
_____

MY **STRATEGY #9** NOTES

MY **STRATEGY #9** NOTES

MY **STRATEGY #9** NOTES

MY **STRATEGY #9** NOTES

MY **STRATEGY #9** NOTES

MY **STRATEGY #9** NOTES

MY **STRATEGY #9** NOTES

ABOUT THE AUTHOR

As a Success Strategist, I help community leaders and moms in business to explore their beliefs and break through the mental blocks that can affect their ability to market their businesses online and offline.

I am an advocate of empowering *"BOSS MOMS"* to stop playing small and show up in their businesses while being active parents.

My unique approach boosts and stimulates moms in business to take strategic action to increase their visibility and be more profitable in their businesses and more active in their communities.

As a mom in business, I have plenty of experience navigating the mental blocks that parenthood and other limiting beliefs can place on businesswomen ready to succeed. With my compelling personal story of putting my success on the back burner to raise my children, I have been inspired to narrow my market to moms in business.

www.ingramcontent.com/pod-product-compliance
Lightning Source LLC
Chambersburg PA
CBHW052056070526
44584CB00017B/2205